Retiring from the civil service after 25 years, William Birmingham worked in policy development and led training courses in the pensions and social security field in Africa, Central Asia and the Caribbean, including living and working for over five years in Beijing. He is a lay minister in the Church of England and is now part of a team running a toddler group in his local church. He also chairs his local Neighbourhood Action Group.

Dedicated to the congregations in Copp, Southampton, Woking, Beijing and Langley, of which I have been a part.

William Birmingham

DIVERSE, CONVERSE AND IN VERSE

Some Scriptural Musings

AUSTIN MACAULEY PUBLISHERS™

LONDON · CAMBRIDGE · NEW YORK · SHARJAH

A CIP catalogue record for this title is available from the British Library.

ISBN 9781398442740 (Paperback)
ISBN 9781398442757 (ePub e-book)

www.austinmacauley.com

First Published 2023
Austin Macauley Publishers Ltd®
1 Canada Square
Canary Wharf
London
E14 5AA

I wish to acknowledge the encouragement that I have received from John and Dalletta Reed, Margaret Nash and Frances Williams to go ahead with this book and the help I have received from Austin Macauley Publishers.

A Birth on Earth of Wondrous Worth

An order went out from the Emperor in Rome
That all should return to their family's home.
Joseph and Mary set off to go down
To their ancestors' home which was Bethlehem town.

They arrived at an inn; Jesus' birth almost due
And begged for a room, any room would them do.
The innkeeper told them, "I regret I'm not able
Every room here is let, but you may use the stable."

So Mary and Joseph then followed the track
That went round the inn to the cave at the back.
And there, midst the cattle, the chickens and corn
As a baby our Saviour, Lord Jesus, was born.

While way down in town all the guests were asleep
Some shepherds were up on the hills keeping sheep.
When suddenly, out of the blackness of night
They were roused from their slumber by a glorious sight.

An angel announced that the Saviour was born
In Bethlehem city that very same morn.
And then with the angel appeared a great choir
Singing glory to God, rising higher and higher.

9

The shepherds then said, "Let's all of us go
To see what has happened in the city below."
They rushed down to Bethlehem ignoring the danger
And found Mary and Joseph and the babe in a manger.

Returning soon after they spread the good news
But had to return to care for their ewes.
Going back to their flocks, it doesn't seem odd
It was shepherds first greeted the true Lamb of God.

A month or two later Mary and Joseph, her spouse
Had moved with the baby back into the house.
When to the surprise of both, greatest and least
A number of visitors arrived from the east.

The visitors, magi, who studied the skies
Were treated by all as especially wise.
A new star had told them a new birth, the news
So they'd come there to worship the King of the Jews.

And setting out with them some presents they'd bring
The first, it was gold, so a gift for a king.
The second was incense, they had brought from the east
A present for worship to give to a priest.

The third of the gifts, myrrh, to bury the dead
The death on the cross in advance this one said.
These presents, all given of significant worth
For the king, priest and dying one's wonderful birth.

Follow the Star

Gold, incense and myrrh.
Gifts for a king and a priest
Who would die for them.

Let Our Voices Exclaim

Love is patient, love is kind
To an insult, love is blind.
Does not envy, does not boast
Love, the giver, gives the most.
Love's not proud, it is not rude
It's not rowdy, it's not lewd.
Not self-seeking, it's polite
In evil it does not delight.
Love which has abundant patience
Rarely shows much irritation.
It does not keep a list of wrongs
Those who do are clanging gongs.
Love rejoices with the truth
And never will do ought uncouth.
Love protects and trusts and hopes
When faced with trouble, always copes.
Love will always persevere
Love as well protects from fear.
If my faith can move a mountain
In a desert spring a fountain.
My assets on the poor I rain
Without that love there's naught I gain.
My body to be burnt, but still
Of benefit to me it's nil.
Prophecies and tongues will pass

But till the end its love will last.
Came the Spirit like a dove
To demonstrate that God is love.
God's love in action we can see
With Jesus dying on the tree.
By faith, no matter who we are,
Amor vincit omnia

Testing, Just Testing

When Jesus was baptised by his cousin, John
The Spirit descended on him like a dove.
A voice he heard came from heaven above
"With Him I'm well pleased, yes, this is my Son."

Straightway the Spirit led Jesus away
To be tempted by Satan for 40 whole days.
When hungry from fasting the accuser then said,
"If you're Son of God, turn these stones into bread."
"Man lives, it is written, not on bread alone
But words," replied Jesus, "from God on his throne."

The devil then took him to the Temple's high crown
And suggested that Jesus should throw himself down.
"For surely," said Satan, "Your angels will care
And make sure that, when falling, will hold you up there."
But Jesus replied, "God's law warns us lest,
We might all be tempted to put God to the test."

The devil took Jesus the whole world to see
"I'll give you it all, if you'll worship me."
And Jesus responded, "O Satan! Depart
And just worship God." Then his ministry did start.

The devil departed at the end of his tempting
A more opportune time this time was pre-empting.
The devil would return which would have been to our loss
By trying to get Jesus to by-pass the cross.

A Calling

James and John beside the sea,
Jesus called them, "Follow me."
Peter and Andrew along there too,
Jesus said, "I'm calling you."
Philip asked to come along,
Brought Nathanael. That's not wrong.

Matthew at the tax man's table,
"Come with me. I know you're able."
Jesus called them all and then,
Told them that they'd soon catch men.
Men and women, children yet,
You can catch them in your net.

Twelve of them became his friends,
Seventy more he then out sends.
Jesus to disciples said,
"Heal the sick and raise the dead."
Disciples sent out each in twos
To tell the world the great good news.
Yet that number is not all,
Today to you he makes a call.
Jesus calls us it to say,
To our neighbours every day.

To follow Jesus must be brave,
As Jesus comes more lives to save.

The Banquet Chief Has a Whine

Jesus' fame had started spreading,
When he was invited to a wedding.
His mother too was a wedding guest,
His disciples also among the rest.

From Cana were the wedding pair,
Nathanael also came from there.
Perhaps with Jesus he's the link,
Soon all the guests began to drink.

After some time, o dear, what doom,
Embarrassment for bride and groom.
The wine they'd ordered – all used up!
Not enough to fill a cup.

Jesus' mother saw the sign,
And said to Jesus, "No more wine."
Jesus answered to his mum,
"Why come to me? My time's not come."
But Mary knew that he could act,
And told the servants with some tact,
"Whatever Jesus says to you,
Whatever he tells you, you must do."

Nearby stood six enormous pots,
Which held of water, an awful lot.
When Jesus spoke they heeded him,
Saying "Fill those pots up to the brim."
And when they'd filled them to the top,
He told them then to take some drops,
Of water out and then instead,
To take them to the banquet's head.

He who knew not whence they came,
Told the groom it was a shame,
Of all the wine that he had passed,
This best wine had been left till last.

"When people need to quench their thirst,
Most people drink the best wine first.
So, when the guests have drunk too much,
Then's not the time to bring out such."

St John includes the Cana story.
To show the Lord revealed his glory.
Turning water into wine,
Was the first of Jesus' signs.

A Hailing,
a Holing and a Healing

Jesus can heal – Do you want some proof?
Then consider the man let down through the roof.
The man was so ill, he was stretched out in bed.
His friends thought that soon the poor man would be dead.

But could they do anything before his life's end?
They did what they could for a true life-long friend.
They'd heard about Jesus and how he could heal.
And if they'd done nothing how badly they'd feel.

They'd carry their sick friend and Jesus then reach.
And hoped that in time they could Jesus beseech.
They came to the house where they heard Jesus teach.
But the crowd was so deep and there wasn't a breach.
They had got to the stage when they began to lose hope.
Until one of them saw a few lengths of rope.
"If we tie up the ropes to the sides of the bed,
We bring him to Jesus by lowering instead."

Though weary from carrying their friend's bed for miles,
They climbed up the stairs and sat down on the tiles.
They tied up the bed to the ropes they had taken,
And hoped that their noise would the owner not waken.
They worked with some fury to undo some tiles,

While Jesus below kept on teaching the while.
And though all their effort had taken its toll,
When they had all finished in the roof was a hole.

They fitted the ropes as was their intent,
And slowly but surely saw their friend's slow descent.
To Jesus' surprise, midway through his talk,
A bed and a patient unable to walk,
Alighted in front of just where he had sat.
And Jesus looked down on the man on the mat.

"Your sins are forgiven," Jesus said to the man.
His friends quickly downstairs to Jesus now ran,
But some of the large crowd who nearby did live,
To Jesus complained, "Only God can forgive!"
But Jesus responded what's better to talk,
"Your sins are forgiven." or "Get up and walk."

And then to the friend Jesus said straight away,
"Please pick up your bed. You can go on your way."
The man then got up and met up with the friends,
Who had carried him there round so many bends.
For all that they'd hoped for, their friend was now healed
And their trust in Christ Jesus for ever was sealed.

Jesus Heals the Body of a Roman Sergeant's Squaddie

A centurion, a sort of Roman NCO,
Equipped to lead his men out to fight whatever foe,
Had come in peace to Jesus seeking healing for his man,
For he believed that no one could, except that Jesus can.
"My servant," said the soldier, "is suffering very badly."
Jesus would have gone with him to heal the man quite
gladly.
Said Jesus to the soldier, "Sir, to heal I'll go straightway."
The man replied, "No, please don't come. The word you just
need say.
For with my rank, the power I have to make the troops obey,
As I have soldiers under me who do just as I say.
They have to follow what I say and must not go astray.
If I say come, the soldier comes; if I say stay, they'll stay.
I have the power to order them with authority from Rome;
But I don't deserve, the soldier said, to ask you to my
home."
Jesus was astounded to hear the soldier's trust,
To heal the sick, he'd always felt to meet with them he must.
He said the word, the man was healed. The Lord did not
refuse,
For greater faith the man had shown than shown so far by
Jews.

A Son-Day and a Son-Rise

Jesus went to Cana where he turned water into wine
And while he was at Cana he performed a second sign.
A VIP whose son was sick heard Jesus had come back
From Jerusalem to Galilee; so set off on the track.
From Capernaum to Cana to ask the healer please
To come back to Capernaum to heal his son's disease.
"Sir, please come to Capernaum or else my child will die."
Jesus told him, "Go back home. Your son will live, not die."
The man believed what Jesus said; what Jesus said he'd
heard,
And straightway set off home again, taking Jesus at his
word.
And returning to Capernaum, met his servants on the way
"Your son will live, he's getting well; the fever's gone
away."
The VIP then questioned them and asked them to recall
The hour the lad got better, when healing had begun.
"The seventh hour, just after lunch," the answer of them all;
"The seventh hour," they all confirmed, when fever left your
son."
The seventh hour, the very hour when Jesus said he'd live
The very hour the VIP his trust in him did give.
He, when back home, first saw his son, so greatly was
relieved,

That he and all his household in Jesus now believed.
Jesus set out on his travels again
And came to a new town whose name it was Nain.
His disciples came with him and also a crowd
But when he arrived met with men with heads bowed
As mourners were taking a lad to his grave.
His mother, a widow, was terribly brave.
Jesus had compassion and told her, "Don't cry."
For the widow had seen her only son die.
Jesus came to the coffin; the bearers stood still.
They waited for Jesus to see what he willed.
"Young man, I tell you now to arise."
The young man sat up, and he opened his eyes
And started to speak to one and another.
Then Jesus returned the lad to his mother.
The people around when this action they saw
Gave praises to God and were all filled with awe.
"A great prophet," they said, "has appeared in our midst.
The Saviour who does all that his Father him bids."

Beyond the Pail

On the way back to Galilee Jesus came first
To a town in Samaria where he suffered from thirst.
He came to where Jacob had provided a well
And what happened next St John starts to tell.
Along came a woman who came water to draw
For fetching the water was for women a chore.
Jesus then asked her to give him a drink.
The woman on hearing him started to think
How Jesus, a Jew, would a Samaritan ask
And any way he'd no pail for the task.
"You've nothing to draw with and the well is quite deep.
If I get you water, for me it's not cheap."

"If you knew," said Jesus, "who'd made the request
You'd ask for his water so you would be blessed,
"To drink from this well, a pail you must bring
But the water I give is a continuous spring.
Those who will drink it will not thirst again."
"Please give me that water so we don't need the rain."

"Go call for your husband and then please come back,"
"But I have no husband. It's something I lack."
"You've had five husbands already who lived in your house
And the one who's now with you, is not really your spouse."
"You are a prophet. On that I can count.

Our forebears have worshiped here long on this mount.
And not in Jerusalem where Jews say to go."
"You Samaritans worship what you do not know.
The time is now coming when all worship be true
To the Father in spirit and in truth also too."
"*Messiah will come and then we all shall see.*"
Said Jesus in response "It is I who am he."

Leaving her water, back to town did she run
And said, "*Come see a man who knew all I have done.*"
What the woman now told them, the townsfolk received
And because of her witness, many townsfolk believed.
The woman turned back and the townsfolk then brought her
To the living Lord Jesus and his living water.
So now if you find you've a spiritual thirst
Please come to the Saviour, the thing to do first.
To come to him's only the one thing you oughta
To drink from the spring of the Lord's living water.

A Well-Bred Lad, a Fishy Story
and Disciples All at Sea

After John the Baptist's death, Jesus crossed the lake.
From preaching and teaching he needed a break
To have for himself a brief time and some space
To spend time with his Father in a solitary place.
But when a huge crowd saw to where he was making
Along the lake shore that direction were taking.
When Jesus arrived, they had got there before
Five thousand men and still probably more.
They'd come to hear Jesus for that's what they did.
Alongside them, too, were the women and kids.

So, Jesus sat down on the edge of the shore
And started to preach and to teach them some more.
When Jesus stopped preaching, got up from a rock
The time had now reached roughly seven o'clock.
The disciples of Jesus then started to say
That Jesus should tell them to go on their way.
They needed to go where to buy food and drink.
And Jesus' reply was – well, what do you think?
You feed them here. Yes, you feed them today
But Philip said it would cost half a year's pay.
But Andrew came forward with only a lad.
He'd offered as food everything that he had.
Five loaves and two fishes were all he had brought

But to give them to Jesus, he felt that he ought.
Jesus took what was offered and started to bless
And what he did next no one present could guess.
He ordered his friends the boy's offering to pass
To the 5,000 folks told to sit on the grass.
And when everyone there had eaten their fill
Of food that remained a lot there was still.

The disciples, all twelve, had to pick up the grains
Filled each of their baskets with all the remains.
When the people all saw what Jesus had done
They thought him the prophet expected to come.
Realizing they wanted a king him to make
He withdrew to a mountain while his friends crossed the
lake.

When the disciples had rowed for three miles or so
And a strong wind against them had started to blow,
The Galilee water had become very rough
And to continue their rowing had become very tough.
Then Jesus approached them; he walked on the lake.
The disciples with terror all started to shake.
But Jesus then told them it was indeed he
So fearful no longer they needed to be.
The disciples were ready to take him on board
And straightway the calm of the lake was restored.

The next day, the crowd on the opposite shore
Discovered that Jesus was with them no more.
And seeing that Jesus had not gone aboard
The only one boat the disciples had moored

Some boats from Tiberias returning they took
To return to Capernaum for Jesus to look.

A Stone Wall Response

Jesus sat in the temple court
To teach, for that is where he taught.
So all could hear, He spoke quite loud
And gathered round him quite a crowd.
Some lawyers and some Pharisees
Approached him with a clever wheeze
To catch him out before the crowd.
And having caught him go back proud.
They came to Jesus with the effrontery
To bring with them a woman who'd
They brought to Jesus and accused.
That she'd been taken in adultery.

"Teacher, in adultery she was found."
But Jesus wrote down on the ground.
"The law commands that she be stoned.
Should we now start stones to be honed?"

To trap him they then asked the Lord
"Good master, what do you record?"
Despite the words they were inciting
Jesus continued with his writing.
At length when they had stopped their questions
Jesus came with his suggestion.

"Which of you, who's without sin.
Should now the stoning first begin?"

Then one by one they slipped away
Their try to catch him gone astray.
The woman found herself alone
With Jesus but without the stones.

"Where are they?" Jesus asked her then
"The group just now of lawyer men?
Is no-one left of your accusers?"
(The men of her would-be abusers)

"Does no-one here condemn you now?"
Said Jesus as he wiped his brow
She replied that there was none.
The lawyers all away had gone.

"And nor do I," said Jesus, as she departed
He sent her on her way warm hearted.
But Jesus did as well implore,
When leaving, she should sin no more.

That the Blind May See

It must be someone's fault he could not see.
Perhaps his parents had displeased the Power beyond the sky
So he had borne the punishment for them, or was it he
Who had offended mighty God on high
To cause his loss of sight?

But he from birth had but his blindness known.
No thought of his, or deed, deserving had been of the loss;
No sin performed by parent, ere conceived was he, the
cause,
But here on earth in him there might be shown
Of God the power and might.

The stranger came and spat upon the path.
With thumb and finger rubbed the spittle in the dusty dry
And made some mud. He rubbed the tacky sludge upon each
eye
And told the beggar, "Go and take a bath
Within Siloam's pool."

The blind man did as had to him been said
And to Siloam which in Hebrew has the meaning 'Sent'
Still blind, by feeling and with bumping into people, went
And drenched himself and washed his head
And eyes in water cool.

He saw – and so did everyone who'd pitched
Their coppers down into the blind man's begging bowl
before.
"Is this the blind man whom we used to see down on the
floor?
Who used to beg?"
"He cannot be the man; for he has eyes which
See."
"That beggar man is me!"

He spoke. But others said, "It looks like him."
"I am the man," he said, "the man who begged, who once
was blind.
The man to whom in poverty you showed that man could
kindness show,
Whose eyes and countenance were dim,
But now my eyes can see."

"How can you see?
By whose device your sight
You have received?"
"The man called Jesus made some mud, to place
It on my eyes. He ordered me to go and wash my face
And eyes within Siloam's pool and light
Streamed through my eyes and soul."

The beggar, called before the Pharisees
Who said that as the day on which the eyes did first have
sight
The Sabbath was, that Jesus who made mud and rubbed the
right

Eye and the left, no man of God could be
For breaking Sabbath law.

"No sinner could perform such signs," some owned,
But others charged the man again to tell them whom he
thought
Had been the one who healed his eyes. "Will you as well be
taught?
By him who is a Prophet, for such alone
Of men could make me whole."

They asked his parents whether he, their son,
Was blind from birth as he had said and how he now could
see.
"He is our son, was blind from birth, but how he sees now,
none
Can answer you, but only there is he
Himself to answer for."

To tell the truth, so help you God, the man
Was forced to swear. "We know this man a sinner is," they
pressed
"For Sabbath by command of God is not for work, but rest."
"Whether a sinner know I not. I can
Though blind from birth now see."

"You follow him. Moses our teacher is.
God spoke to Moses on high Sinai's mount, but Jesus we
Do not know whence has come."
"How odd you do not know whence he
Who healed me is, for God has answered his

Own word. For now I see.
None but a man of God could do a sign
Which he has done." Confirming he a sinner was from birth
They sent him from the synagogue, a man of little worth.
But Jesus came the outcast man to find
And of him to request,

"Do you believe now in, my friend, the Son
Of Man?"
"Tell me, sir, who he is that I may so believe?"
"Him you have seen and now he talks with you."
"Lord, I believe."
And saying so, he knelt before the one
Alone at whose behest,

The scales had fallen from before each eye.
"I came into this world an arbiter of all to be,
That those who see be blind and those who are yet blind
should see."
"You can't," they said, "mean blindness yet have I?
"Guilty you still will be,
Because you claim to see."

Thugs, Mugs and Samaritan Hugs

A man went down to Jericho
His merchandise to sell.
And going from Jerusalem
Some brigands on him fell.
The robbers beat and wounded him.
They punched him on his head.
And then they stole his goods away
And left him almost dead.

A priest went down to Jericho
And to the man drew nigh.
He hurried on his way and on
The other side passed by.
A Levite also came that way
And feared the man had died.
But glancing briefly where he lay,
Passed by the other side.

Another man passed by that way,
Samaritan was he.
He stopped his beast beside the spot
The injured man to see.
He looked upon him lying there
Of life barely a sign.

He placed him on his donkey's back
And poured in oil and wine.

The Good Samaritan then took
The poor man to an inn.
And waited there to care for him
Till healing should begin.
And when, at last, he had to go
Some money to the host
He gave to care for him. "Now which
A neighbour proved the most?"

Asked Jesus then of him who asked
"My neighbour who is he?"
"The one," his questioner replied,
"Who showed the man mercy."
Then Jesus turned and said to him
"Go now and do as he."
The same instruction Jesus gives
As well to you and me.

Bed, Bread and a Visitor Fed

You're tucked up in bed and there's a knock on your door.
A fright at midnight
The knocking continues and you hear a loud shout.
"Go away," you say.
Your door bell is rung and of shouting there's more.
The shout. "Come out."
Your neighbour is calling, not some drunken lout.
"I've said I'm in bed.

"You've woken my wife and the kids now are crying.
They're awake. For goodness sake.
I've asked you already; o please go away.
We're weary; eyes bleary."
The knocking continues; the shouting and sighing.
"Come down."
I frown.
"Tomorrow I'll help you; in bed I'm now lying.
By day; it's OK."

"O please will you help me; my friend has just come
What an oaf; I've no loaf.
We kept back the rice that we had in the house
Instead we ate bread.
We've nothing to give him. I must seem so dumb
There's just a crust.

That's why I'm knocking I hoped you to rouse
To borrow before tomorrow."

At length, the house owner agrees to get up.
He cares. Goes downstairs
Takes bread from his diet to get back to some quiet.
Kids asleep; not a peep.
Gives the neighbour three loaves and of water a cup.
Just sufficient – not deficient.
"Tomorrow," he said, "I can urgently buy it.
That's bread," he said.

The householder got up as a result of the noise
Insistent, persistent.
He helped out his neighbour to stop the commotion
Gave bread instead.
Concerned as he was for the sleep of his boys
Their number need slumber.
His kind act ensured that despite his emotion
He gave to save.

The man in the story got up in the night
From his bed to give bread.
As a result of persistence and his neighbour's insistence
Man next door given more.
But Jesus contrasted with God who does right
Knock the door – God gives more
No need for insistence – be simply persistent
No wait – on a plate.
You may be hungry for spiritual bread
Just ask – no hard task.

You want to be living – you're spiritually dead.
Just pray; start today.
And God waits to answer and give you that life
With leaven to heaven.
And God wants to answer and take away strife
From you; that's who.

Ewe and You – Lost, Found and a Couple of Pounds

A shepherd is employed to keep
A flock of very silly sheep.
He finds them grass and water too
For that is what all shepherds do.

Now one day shepherd made a line
But counted only ninety-nine.
He should have had a hundred through
But found that he had lost a ewe.

His job it was the flock to mind
But he set off the one to find
And when he found her, he rejoiced
And on his shoulder the ewe did hoist.

And God is like that with his sheep.
For everyone he wants to keep.
He goes to search for any lost.
For Jesus it was at a cost.

Jesus endured the cross of shame
So you and I could bear his name.
So as a shepherd seeks a ewe
The good one seeks to find you too.

A woman who has lost some pounds
Will search the house until they're found –
Behind the chairs, beneath the bed
And even in the garden shed.

And when she finds them, search now ends;
Rejoicing calls up all her friends.
Rejoice with me, please come around
For what I lost I now have found.

When you've been lost, but then are found
God's angels sing a joyful round.
A special song; it's quite intense
For every sinner who repents.

Some Dark Clouds and the Son

Hey, Dad
What, lad?
Your will's been set,
Give me now what I'll get.
Being on the farm I'm bored
I want to see some life abroad
I don't want to waste time here
When I can enjoy a great gap year.
Son, please stay. I'll do my best
I will not put you to the test.
I have every faith in you
Wherever you go whatever you do.
But stay
Don't go away just making hay.
No, father.
To go I'd rather.
I want some life
May find a wife
I won't be bad
So don't be sad.
His dad was fair
He got his share.
And with the kitty
He hit the city.

He lived life with his mates
With girls he had dates.
He drew from his bank
And each night they drank.
They gambled a lot
And even smoked pot.
And when he was high
What a popular guy.
But their friendship was a con
When his money had all gone.
They didn't want to know
When he'd used up all his dough.
He'd paid for them while he had still had a mint
They left him alone once he'd become skint.
To him it seemed to be funny
He'd paid when he had money.
Now he had none
He was left out of the fun.

When famine arose, it came to the crunch.
He'd nothing to eat for his dinner or lunch.
With no food to eat and nothing to buy it
He had to make do with a minimal diet.
To find food for himself either he had to rob
Or go out to find him a suitable job.
At length he found work by caring for pigs
With income too little to pay for his digs.
And you can really imagine the scene
He's forced to eat only the pig swill and beans.

He came to himself and then had a thought
To go to his father was the thing that he ought.
His father had plenty to drink in his tub
Each day his workers were given their grub,
Sufficient and plenty with the rest to be binned.
I'll return to my father and say I have sinned.
Please Father do take me but not as a son
I'll work as your servant until all is done.

His father for years had looked out for the lad
To see him returning the father was glad.
He rushed out to meet him with pleasure not half
And ordered the killing of a young fatted calf,
For the son whose return had now become real,
To prepare for a feast at a celebratory meal

At this point his brother returned to the farm
And hearing the jollity raised an alarm.
"Your brother's come back – yes now he's returned
Your father's rejoicing and the calf's being burned."
That brother then stated he would not come in
To welcome a brother whose life had been sin.
His father rebuked him and had to explain
His brother had sinned but had come home again.
Though the elder had done on the farm every task
As son he would have everything he could ask.
As family, father and brother were bound
To welcome a sibling once lost, but now found.

And you who've been lost and been caught up in sin
Who wish to repent and return to the Lord

Live life not in sin but instead you would rather
Come back to the Lord and meet with the Father.
Remember the Father who wants you restored
To forgive your past faults and so welcome you in.

He Gave Us Eyes to See Them

The rich man in his castle
The poor man at his gate
God made them to be holy
At death they met their fate.

The rich man went to Hades
The poor man went instead
To stay alongside Abraham
Where he would find a bed.

The rich man begged for cooling
Down from the poor man's state.
The patriarch advised him
His request was made too late.

"Then send one to my brothers
And warn them of my fate.
To let them show repentance
Before it is too late."

"They haven't heeded Moses;
The prophets they've ignored.
If someone rises from the dead…
They'd not believe the Lord."

The rich man in his castle;
The poor man in the street.
It's time to help the latter
By giving food to eat.

When you receive a blessing
And wish to show your thanks,
Just buy some extra items
To give to your food bank.

All things bright and beautiful
All people great or small
Whether rich or penny-less
The Lord God loves us all.

The Sower Sows Some Seeds in Some Sundry Sorts of Soils

One man went to sow, went to sow a meadow;
One man and his dog went to sow a meadow.
Some seed fell on the path, the path along the meadow.
Some people trod it down, and birds on it they fed-o.

Some seed fell on the rock, the rock below the meadow.
It sprouted first, the roots dried out, the plants they soon
wilted-o.
Some seed fell in the thorns, which covered up the meadow;
The thorns grew up and choked the plants and they soon
became dead-o.
Some seed fell on good soil, the best bit of the meadow,
Produced a crop, a hundredfold which men then harvested-o.

The Word of God is sown, is sown in you and me-o.
We hear the Word, and will it grow? We'll have to wait and
see-o.
Some hear the Word of God. The Devil comes for stealing.
They lose the Word, they don't believe and don't get any
healing.
Some hear the Word of God. They first receive it gladly.
It takes no root. When testing comes, they rush away quite
madly.

Some hear the Word of God. Their lives are full of other
Cares and pleasures, riches too, which God's Word quickly
smother.
Some hear the Word of God. It grows and deeply rooted.
They keep it in a tender heart and very soon they've fruited.

Sow What

One man went to sow some seeds within his meadow.
His enemy then sowed some weeds which then grew up
together.
The sower's servants asked the man, shall we the weeds now
gather.
The man replied that they should not, but let them grow
together.
When harvest came the sower then unto the reapers said-o
Collect the weeds and bundle them and burn them till
they're dead-o.
And then collect the full-grown wheat from which to make
the bread-o.
For then we'll grind the wheat to flour from which we'll all
be fed-o.
Said Jesus then to all his friends the world is like the
meadow.
The evil one has sown the weeds, like sinners who'll be
dead-o
The righteous then the angels will, just like a harvest
spread-o,
Collect them up, and then they'll shine just as the Lord has
said-o.

Sheep and Goats

I ended up homeless; you gave me a bed.
I ended up starving; you gave me some bread.
I became dehydrated; you made me some tea
Whatever I needed, you offered to me.

I ended up homeless; I slept on the street.
I ended up starving; I'd nothing to eat.
I became dehydrated; was violently sick
And when you walked past me, you gave me a kick.

I lost my employment: our lives were a mess,
You gave me some trousers and my girlfriend a dress.
When sickly you took me to see A&E
And waited behind until they had seen me.

I lost my employment: you gave me no job,
For some clothes to wear, I just had to rob.
When sickly you told me that I shouldn't fuss
I could get to the hospital on the hospital bus.

When lying in hospital, I became very bored
But you came to visit and cheered up the ward.
When I was imprisoned, you showed me you care
You went out of your way to visit me there.

When lying in hospital, I became very bored
But you didn't come as you knew not which ward.
When I was imprisoned, you didn't dare
Come into the prison to visit me there.

Lord, when did I save you from a terrible fate?
When did I see you in such a bad state?
You might not have noticed, but I still could see
As you did it for him, you did it for me.

Lord, when did I leave you to such a bad fate?
When did I see you in such a bad state?
You might not have noticed, but I still could see
As you didn't for him, you didn't for me.

The King will divide the sheep from the goats.
He's seen what you've done and has taken a note.
For those who took action there's a place in his court
But no place for those giving others no thought.

You's and Kids

Are you a one who'll bring kids to the Lord?
For him to lay hands on and pray?
Or are you a one who will drive them away?
Though Jesus wants children aboard.

For unless you become like a wee little bairn
You won't enter the kingdom of God.
For the greatest within the kingdom of heaven
Has come in like a child – how odd.

If you are the one to cause children to sin
And to lead any child such a life to begin,
'Twere better said Jesus that a millstone should be
Tied round your neck and you drowned in the sea.

Greed, a Feed and
a Need to Heed

Someone asked Jesus to tell the man's brother
To split their inheritance 'tween him and the other.
Jesus replied to the man in his fury
He'd not been appointed their judge or their jury.

Jesus then taught at the start of a session
A man's life should not consist of possessions.
Instead we all need at once to take heed
That we don't become obsessive with greed.

The field of a farmer produced a return.
He wondered how best to increase what he earned.
His trouble was that if he grew a lot more
He'd nowhere in which the surplus to store.

At length he decided just what he would do;
He'd tear down his barns and build others anew.
The barns would be bigger – of that he'd be sure
So they would be able to hold a lot more.

His profit would increase – he'd no need to labour
For anything needed he'd employ his neighbour.
Each evening before supper, he'd drink port or sherry.
Why work now when he could eat, drink and be merry.

Though he seemed to think him a right clever bod
He'd left from the equation the thinking of God.
For God said the right to his life was required;
Instead of the merriment his life would expire.

From the work he had done and the barns he had built
The riches he'd gained with no feeling of guilt
He'd not reap the benefit, his work was in vain.
So he from his actions had nothing to gain.

For God had declared that the man was a fool;
To gain more in greed he broke one golden rule
Which many today will still think it odd
That we in our life must be rich unto God.

The Mustard Seed

Mustard seed size faith,
Orders a mountain to move.
It obeys and moves.

Mustard seed though small,
Grows into a massive tree.
Birds can perch in it.

The birds of the air,
Need not sow or reap or store.
But by God are fed.

A Side-On Request

Jesus withdrew to the region of Sidon
And there he was met by a woman who cried on –
Though being a Canaanite, was not a Jew
But still she believed in what Jesus could do.
"Lord, Son of David, have mercy," she wailed,
"My daughter by demons is being assailed."

To all her appealing, Jesus said not a word
But the disciples who with him the woman had heard
Indignant that she had got in their way
Urged Jesus to send the woman away.
"I was sent only to Israel's lost sheep,"
Said Jesus, the woman beginning to weep.

"Lord, help me," the woman then begged on her knees
And Jesus then answered in response to her pleas,
"It's not right to take up the children's own bread
And toss it away to their doggies instead."

"Yes, Lord," she answered as quick as was able.
"The dogs eat the food that drops off from the table."
"You have great faith. I will grant your appeal."
From that very hour her daughter was healed.

Two Men Say Amen

Two men one day went up to pray.
The Pharisee did so every day.
He was there right on the dot.
And always at the self-same spot.

The other was a tax collector.
Many there would not suspect a
Man like him would come to pray,
Who forced the folk their tax to pay.

The Pharisee, with words off pat,
Was proud in front of others when,
O God, he prayed I thank you that,
I'm not at all like other men.

He looked around and with relief,
Told God he never was a thief.
And as his prayer began to roll on,
He pointed out he'd never stolen.

I've done no bad things in my life,
And never cheated on my wife.
He turned around and looking at,
The other praying bureaucrat.

Said no way am I like that man,
With what I do and what I am.
I can approach the Lord in prayer.
With what he is I doubt he dare.

Throughout my present and my past,
I've twice a week fulfilled a fast.
And when I get some pay or rent,
Of that I give the ten per cent.

The other prayed as a beginner,
Just looked down and beat his breast,
And prayed what was for him his best,
Have mercy, Lord, I am a sinner.

The tax man's prayer came from the heart.
The other thought that he was smart.
Jesus the Pharisee decried,
The other went home justified.

But Don't Tell Anyone

"Jesus, Rabbi, Please come quick,
My little daughter's very sick.
I've come to you because I feel,
That you're the one with power to heal."
The crowd around were all agog –
A ruler of the synagogue,
Had come to beg with such deep feeling,
Jesus for his daughter's healing.
Before the Master Jairus bowed,
In front of all the Jesus' crowd.

Jesus at once along the road,
To Jairus' house then quickly strode.
He kept on walking on until,
All at once he stood quite still.

"Who has touched me?" Jesus spoke.
Peter thought it was a joke.
"The crowd keeps bumping into you.
It's no good asking which or who."
But one had touched his garment's rim
He'd felt some power go out from him.
A woman who'd been ill for years,
Had tried to hide because of fear.
She'd touched his cloak to get his healing

But, once found out, before him kneeling,
The woman started to explain.
She'd lived for 12 years all in pain.
She spent her all on doctors' bills,
But now of savings she had nil.
She'd had a bleed for 12 whole years,
But meeting Jesus calmed her fears.
Jesus gave what she was needing.
Touching Jesus stopped her bleeding.
Knowing it no longer bled,
Jesus turned to her and said,
It was her faith that enabled healing.
Being healed that faith was sealing.
As the bleeding now had ceased,
Jesus told her, "Go in peace."

Meanwhile Jairus much concerned,
At Jesus causing a delay.
From one of his household shortly learned,
His daughter had since passed away.
When Jesus set off to go faster,
They said no longer trouble the Master.
Jesus replied, "Don't be afraid."
As Jairus with the Master stayed.
"Believe," said Jesus, "Trust in me.
For your daughter, healed will be."

Arriving at the ruler's house,
He told the wailers not to cry.
The wailers thought that he'd no nous,
To say she'd wake up by and by.

"For she's asleep; she is not dead,"
Was what the healer to them said.
At this the wailers simply laughed,
Believing Jesus' words were daft.

Jesus took Peter, James and John,
The girl's two parents followed on.
No one else allowed to come.
But Jesus, disciples, Dad and Mum.
Around the bed they took a stand,
He took the daughter by the hand.
And to her Dad's and Mum's surprise,
Said, "Little girl, please now arise."
Her spirit now to her returned.
She sat up and to parents turned.
"Give her something now to eat."
Presumably it was a treat.

You Are the One

Jesus and his friends drew near
To Philip's town of Caesarea.
Jesus who of God the Lamb
Asked them who folks say I am.
Some – the Baptist come alive
Others – Elijah (who did strive
Before King Ahab and was bold),
Or else a prophet from days of old.

"But who do you say that I am?"
Said Peter to God's Son, the Lamb,
"You are the Christ, God's only Son;
You are the long expected one."

"Blessed are you, o son of John
For this was not revealed by man,
Not by flesh and blood, but by
My Father, God, who reigns on high.

For you are Peter. On this rock
I'll build my church, withstand a shock.
It will be safe and will be well,
Not overcome by gates of hell."

"I give to you the kingdom's keys.
What you seize on earth in heaven is seized.
What you loose on earth is loosed above,"
Said Jesus who is God of love.

Another Wall of Jericho

At Jericho had stood a wall.
When Joshua's trumpets made a call
That wall at once began to fall
    On the Jericho Road.

"Why the hubbub? Why the crowd?"
Asked the beggar blind and cowed.
Then at once he shouted loud,
    On the Jericho Road.

Bartimaeus, it was he,
Sure the Lord could make him see.
"Son of David, mercy on me."
    On the Jericho Road.

"Lord, I would receive my sight."
Jesus met him in his plight.
All at once he saw the light
    On the Jericho Road.

Zacchaeus next, a taxman he,
The miracle worker wished to see.
Short, he had to climb a tree
    On the Jericho Road.

Passing close by Jericho town
Jesus called him to come down.
Many folk began to frown
On the Jericho Road.

"I tonight with you must stay."
"Half I give the poor this day;
If ought I swindled, I'll repay"
On the Jericho Road.

Twixt God and man sin caused a wall
Till man responds to Jesus' call.
Straightway the barrier starts to fall
On the Jericho Road.

4Give 490X

Said Peter to Jesus, "So what if my brother,
I find out at inception
Alongside another
Performed some deception.
How many times should I seek to forgive?
As together we both have our lives here to live.
I think that the number should be up to seven.
Is that what's expected by all up in heaven?"
Jesus replied that what's wanted in heaven
Is to forgive him instead as at seventy times seven.

Work Today, Receive Your Pay, Then Say Hey!!

Jesus talked about a donor
Who also was a vineyard owner.
To pick the grapes he could not stop
So sought someone to pick his crop.

And walking through the village when
He came across a group of men.
"Please come and work for me all day
The proper wage for work I'll pay."

To take the job the men were quick
And quickly started grapes to pick.

Three hours later at roughly ten
The owner came to town again
And passing by the market then
To his surprise were yet more men.

Please come and work for me today
The proper wage to you I'll pay.
To take the job these men were quick
And straightway started grapes to pick.

At twelve o'clock and then at three
To other men, "Come work for me.
If to work for me you'll stay
The proper wage to you I'll pay."

And when it came to half past five
When at the market he arrived
He found that there were still some boys
Who hoped to find some apt employ.

"I ask you now, so could you say
Why you have stood here all the day?"
"Standing here we all are tired
But no-one came, so we weren't hired."

"Till dark there's only just an hour
Please come and work for all the rest
And start at once, I ask you, lest
There just might be a heavy shower."

When darkness fell, the workers came
And lined up in an ordered queue
And to the owner gave their name.
And details of their picking too.

Payment went first to those who were recent
For working one hour their money was decent.
Then those who had worked three hours or more
Expected to be paid an awful lot more.
But each of the workers when he gave his name
Was given as wages exactly the same.

Those who'd worked longer began to complain
They'd worked there much longer, so more they should gain.

The owner then told them he'd not been unfair
Instead he'd been generous to each of them there.
They'd each received payment that they had agreed
He'd paid them a sum far more than he need.

He ended up thinking that it seemed a bit funny
That workers should question how he used his money.
For God in his mercy welcomes all who repent
However their previous lifetime was spent.
For Jesus explained for the best and the worst
That the first shall be last and the last shall be first.

Two Brothers and Others

James, the disciple, and John, James's brother,
Requested the Lord, with Salome, their mother,
That Jesus would do a particular thing
Once Jesus had entered his kingdom as king.

"When you in your power, sit down on your throne
Could we sit beside you on seats of our own?
With one of us sat on the chair to your right,
The other your left, at an appropriate height."

Jesus replied that to do so he can't.
For positions like these were his Father's to grant.
He'd asked whether they could drink of his cup
They said that they could – they would drink it all up.

The other disciples, learning what they'd requested,
Were exceedingly cross, their request they detested.
Jesus called all the twelve, including the brothers,
Saying Gentiles do lord it, but they should do other.

"Whoever among you desires to be great,
Must first take the role of a servant and wait."
The disciples had Jesus who on them did serve
And serves us today which we don't deserve.

While at the last supper, he washed all their feet
Despite an objection from Simon called Pete.
Jesus said that without it Peter wouldn't be clean.
So Peter said wash head, feet and all in between.

Today we are called to serve God and our neighbour
To love them and willingly for them to labour.
On the cross Jesus' life paid a ransom for many
Without him there'd be no salvation for any.

Let us Jesus' ministry closely observe
And learn from it, now how best we can serve.

Two Other Brothers

A farmer had two strapping lads
Who, trained they were, to work for Dad.
Said Dad to elder brother, Joe,
To pick the grapes it's time to go.
Said Joe, "I'll set off right away,
Continue picking all the day."
Said Dad to younger brother, Jim,
"It's time for you to follow him."
Said Jim to Father, "I won't go.
I've more important things, you know."

But brother Joe was wont to shirk
So did not go to do the work.
Meanwhile the younger brother Jim's
Own conscience got the better of him.
What he had planned to do, he dropped
And all day long he never stopped.

Which brother, Jesus asked the throng
Had done what's right and which what's wrong?
The crowd then pointed to the one
Though saying, No! The work had done.
And as they looked at brother Jim
They all agreed that it was him
Jesus replied, "Tax men and whores

Place in God's kingdom precedes yours.
When God had John the Baptist sent
They'd listened and did then repent."

Widows Might

Jesus in the temple saw
A widow who was very poor.
Who put a pair of coins within
The temple's main collecting tin.

Beside the widow Jesus saw
Some wealthy givers of much more.
They all hoped that they'd be feted
Because of all that they'd donated.

Quite quietly the widow gave
The pair of coins that she had saved.
Of her said Jesus, "She has given
More than them in sight of heaven.

She has given all she had;
For them it cost them just a tad.
They will gain their satisfaction
But God will recognize her action."

Jesus gave for us his all.
Do we give back only what's small?
If we don't give back what is right,
Perhaps we'll find that widows might.

Architecture

God told Noah, Build an ark.
Build with wood without the bark.
For I'm going to make it rain
It will flood across the plain.
If you build it, you will see
In the ark, quite safe you'll be.

Noah got some pitch and wood,
Built the ark as best he could.
Then God spoke from out of heaven
Get some creatures, pairs of seven.
Other creatures, two by two
Till the ark looked like a zoo.

Noah then he climbed aboard,
Obedient was he to the Lord.
Wife and family got in too
That's what God had said to do.
Once aboard, the rain came down.
In the ark they did not drown.

Forty days the rain did fall
Till the water covered all.
In the ark they had to stay
Till the water drained away.

After days, Noah thought he oughta
Check if the ground's still under water.
To learn, a raven he sent out.
It came back empty just about.
Then he waited just a week
And sent a dove once more to seek.
The dove returned back to the ark
With an olive leaf without the bark.
To understand what the leaf had meant
Another week the bird was sent.
This time the dove did not return
From which old Noah now would learn.
That Noah's family at last
Had reached dry land; the flood was past.

God made a covenant, when dry,
As sign, a rainbow in the sky,
That, though the Lord would make it rain,
He'd never flood the earth again.

Jesus quoted Noah's ark;
As a warning it is stark.
Despite the warning folks instead
Still eat and drink and also wed.
Before the Son of Man returns,
From Noah's ark few will have learned.

God who saved the ark's whole crew
Wants to save both me and you.
Save us from the world of sin;
Bring us where it says way in

To where God wants both you and me
Evermore with him to be.

A Treasure Discovered

With a metal detector you may find a hoard
Of gold or of silver of a king or a lord.
Dropped there by accident, or placed by a donor
The value's half yours and half the land's owner
But you want the total – it's worth a great price.
If you owned the land, you'd have double – how nice.
So you don't tell the owner the hoard that you've found
Until he has sold you the hoard's bit of ground.

Jesus said something about the kingdom of God.
No metal detector, but a man gave a prod.
And found there a treasure worth millions of pounds
And stayed till he'd bought where the treasure was found.
He determined to buy up the field all around.
He sold all he had so he could buy up the ground.
Said nothing about it till the sale had gone through.
But then went and dug up the treasure anew.

Will you like the man work to buy up the treasure?
A treasure you'll get that's beyond any measure?
The treasure you'll find is no dagger nor sword
It's Jesus you'll have as your Saviour and Lord.
Have you ever thought – this may you astound –
That you are the treasure that Jesus has found.
He's given up all; did at Calvary die

So by death and his rising, it's you he could buy.
And now you are his in the Kingdom of God
To think you're his treasure – now that does seem odd –
He went to the cross so that you could be bought
And with him to heaven he you will have brought

Suppose They Held a Feast but Nobody Came

The King sent his servants north, south, west and east
To invite all the gentry to his son's wedding feast.
Despite invitations, the king then did send
The people invited declined to attend.
One, whom invited, to the King's servant said
That he couldn't come as he'd recently wed.
He considered that if he went away from his wife
He'd regret it throughout the rest of his life.
Another invitee had just bought a cow
To milk it a milkmaid would show him just how.
Another invitee had just bought a field
He needed to view it; his purchase now sealed.
A fourth had procured of oxen five yokes
And to work them and yoke them was no kind of joke.
The King, when it finally got to the stage
That no one would come, flew into a rage.
He ordered the servants to go into the street
And force all to come in to fill every seat.
The King then commanded them to go to the highways
And bring in as guests those that they found in the byways
The servants went out and then only ceased
When the King they'd assured, they'd be full at the feast.
The King for the banquet became so obsessed
When he saw that a guest was improperly dressed.

Instead of the man wearing clothes for a wedding
The King thought he looked as if wearing some bedding.
When challenged as to why he'd not come in a suit.
The embarrassed invitee could only stay mute.
He'd come to the feast where the servants had guided
But not warn the clothes that the King had provided
The King felt he'd insulted the bridegroom and bride
And ordered the servants to throw him outside.
Outside there'd be weeping and gnashing of teeth
As he's thrown out of the kingdom into darkness beneath.

Due Diligence

The work of a couple once took them away
From home, so some months away they must stay
They left some cash – o yes, they did
To support their teen and twenty-age kids.
They hoped to see how much they'd make.
The kids thought this a piece of cake.

The first received a full 5 k
To live on while they were away.
The second got 200 smackers
To prove that she was not a slacker.
Although it seemed a bit absurd
100 quid went to the third

When Mum and Dad to home returned
They asked them how they'd used the cash
You used it well or made a hash?
And how much more you each have earned?

The eldest son to them explained
From IT work – 5k he'd gained
And when he told them what he'd done
His parents praised their industrious son.

Next to speak was his younger sister,
She had worked as a barista…
Explaining what each day she did.
In tips she'd made 200 quid.
The parents then commended daughter
She had done just what she oughta!

To both these kids, their parents said
As both of them had earned their bread
That as the work they'd taken for
They'd be put in charge of plenty more.

Last of all there came the third.
His explanation seemed absurd,
He had taken his 100 pounds
And buried them within the ground.
In the ground he'd made a hole in
Which to ensure it was not stolen.

His parents said in quite a bellow
That he was an idle fellow.
Even if he'd not found work
That was not a ground to shirk.
He should have placed it with a bank
Instead, its value simply shrank.

His father said and then his mother
Said give his money to the others

Jesus told a similar story with a not-too-different ending
The meaning of the story you may now be comprehending!

Ten Little Bridesmaids

Ten little bridesmaids sitting in the gloom,
Ten little bridesmaids waiting for the groom.
Suddenly it's shouted the bridegroom is in sight,
Ten little bridesmaids begin their lamps to light.

Five little bridesmaids had brought with them some oil,
Five others without it their wedding feast would spoil.
This second group of bridesmaids some oil sought from the
rest,
To let them light their lamps so they could enter as a guest.

The other group of bridesmaids refused to give them any,
Saying shops selling oil in the town were two a penny.
Without it till the bridegroom comes you may make a fuss,
But, if we give you some of ours, we've not enough for us.

The second group of bridesmaids then rushed off to the
town,
But while they'd gone, the bridegroom came and with the
rest went down.

Into the wedding banquet room and joined the wedding
feast,
With all the guests and bridesmaids there, with greatest and
with least.

As soon as all the guests had come, the bridegroom locked
the gate,
The second group of bridesmaids then returned a little late.

They came up to the wedding hall and battered on the door,
Please let us in; we're sorry but of oil we needed more.

They shouted to the bridegroom who answered to them
"No,"
The door stayed locked; he said to them, "For you I do not
know."
Jesus used this parable that we on watch should stay,
Of his return we do not know the hour or the day.

A Pack of Tenants

A man planted a vineyard for grapes to make some wine.
He built a wall around it to protect the growing vines.
He put up there a watch tower when the vines produced
some shoots.
And dug a pit for a winepress for crushing all the fruit.

He set off on a journey and to a far place went.
So, he let out his vineyard to some farmers at a rent.
When harvest came, he sent his man to collect some of the
fruit.
The farmers wanting all the crop, gave the owner's man the
boot.

Another man was sent to them to get the owner's share.
The tenants then attacked him and beat him something spare.
A third man came. They treated him in every way the same.
And sent him back to the owner. No further servant came.

At length the owner wondered what else he now could do.
He'd send his son, the son he loved, to that unruly crew.
The tenants put their heads together and came up with a
wheeze.
If we kill off the son and heir the inheritance we seize.

So, when the son at last arrived to take his father's share.

They gathered round the owner's only son and heir.

The tenants met him at the gate and took him back outside.

They punched him and they stabbed him until at last he died.

Jesus asked the people who were standing where he'd
spoken.

What the man would do to them, as the tenants each had
broken.

All the obligations placed on them when they took out the
let.

He would come to kill them, other tenants he would get.

The teachers of the law could see that all that Jesus said.

Was applicable to all of them and so they wanted Jesus dead.

But, frightened of the people, they feared to make arrest.

But the Son of God himself would be the one for sin
oppressed.

3 Siblings and the Third Came Forth

Lazarus was the brother
Of sisters, Martha and another.
While the other sister, Mary, sat enthralled at Jesus' feet,
Sister Martha in the kitchen was preparing food to eat.
Said Martha then to Jesus,
It certainly would ease us
If you, Lord, told my sister
In the kitchen I have missed her.
But Jesus then replied,
Mary chose the better side.
From her it won't be taken
Even if their life is shaken.

Their family life began to shake
When Lazarus to his bed did take.
When next day he in bed was still
The sisters realised that he was ill.
They sent to Jesus, 'Our brother's sick,
Lord, please, we beg you, come here quick.
His disciples all were quite amazed
Jesus stayed put for two whole days,
Despite their plea did not attend
Straightway to come and heal his friend.
To his disciples and for their sake

He said he'd go his friend to wake.
'If he's asleep, he should recover.'
But Jesus said it was the other.
What sisters both had come to dread,
Jesus said, 'Our friend is dead.'
When Jesus came, the house in gloom,
Lazarus was in the tomb.
Martha said in an aside,
'If you had come, he'd not have died.'
Mary, when she quickly came
Said to Jesus just the same.
Said Jesus then among the strife,
"I am the resurrection and the life."
They took Jesus, who had come to save
And brought him to their brother's grave.
Before the tomb Lord Jesus wept,
Removed the stone the entrance kept.
Then Jesus with a mighty shout
Instructed Lazarus to come out.
The brother to sisters was restored
At the order of the Lord.

Some days later at a meal
Mary showed her love was real.
She left the table and she went
And fetched a jar of costly scent.
And poured it over Jesus' feet
It made the whole house smell so sweet.
Mary then before all there
Wiped Jesus' feet with her own hair.
Disciple Judas began to moan

Jesus said, "Leave her alone.
The nard she had to me applied
She'd kept to pour for when I died."

Death and Life

He would not have died.
Had you come here earlier.
"Lazarus, come out!"

"Tabitha arise!"
So Dorcas opened her eyes
And sat up alive.

The door is narrow.
Try to pass through while you can
Before it is closed.

Sin's wages is death.
God's gift is Life Eternal
Through Lord Jesus Christ.

We buried with Christ,
Raised in his resurrection.
Now alive to God.

Use Your Loaf

You'll set off in your car and then you will park it
Within a big car park at a close supermarket.
You're going to buy food and especially some bread
So that when you get home your kids can be fed.
You pick up a trolley and set out on a quest
To buy what you need and make sure it's the best.
You pass through the passage where food is for health
And then reach the part where there's bread on the shelf.
And this is the time when you've got to choose
Which sort of bread is the one you will use.
There's white bread and brown bread and bread made from
rye
And you then will question, "Which bread should I buy?"
And then there's baguettes, the bread come from France
With that for your breakfast, the meal will enhance.
Then there's the shop worker who looks a bit shifty
As he tries to sell you a large 50-50.
Perhaps you could solve it by buying some buns
And there, come from Bath, are some sweet Sally Lunns.
Instead you could buy some yeast and some dough
And make some with water or at least have a go.
Oh, there on the shelf is a packet of baps
They would be good for filling up gaps.
Alternatively there is a packet of cobs
I'm sure for your needs they are right just the job.

Perhaps you could buy just a few little rolls
Or buy a huge loaf made from wheat that is whole.
Oh, there's a small loaf that appears to be nutty
That would be fine for a cheese or ham butty.
And then there's a barm-cake. That would be fine
But could we use that when we take bread and wine?
And when you left home, you're sure someone said
Could you please bring me home a small currant bread?
And just over there there's something you seek
That bread – what's it called? You know it is Greek.
A quiet pitter-patter from someone ahead
Reminds you at last that it's called pitta bread.
And what do you need if you're holding a party?
Perhaps you should get some naan and chapati.
It's taken you now about half an hour
Perhaps you should have bought the yeast and the flour.
And why did it go round and round in your head?
Why, simply, do you find such different breads?
On leaving the store you recall Jesus said
"I am the true and the real living bread."
You can eat all the bread that you've bought from the store
But tomorrow you'll have to go back for some more.
But the bread Jesus gives you will never run out.
You can feed on it always in faith or in doubt.
You will never go hungry if on Jesus you've fed
And you will be filled if you eat that true bread.
The people asked Jesus for a miraculous sign
And Jesus referred them to bread and to wine.
Not Moses, but God, who gave manna so sweet
But Jesus himself is the bread you should eat.
Alone with disciples Jesus took up the bread

"This is my body," Jesus then to them said.
And taking the wine he said, "This is my blood."
The blood would be shed to treat sinners as good.
So, Heavenly Father, so we can be fed
Please give us this day, Lord, our own daily bread.

Cross, Across and a Cross

Behold here comes of Kings, the King.
Lay down your cloaks and palm fronds bring.
And yet he comes not on a horse,
Nor with a military force.
He rides up seated on an ass,
Surrounded by of folk a mass.
A noisy crowd, they break off palms.
Which to the powerful brings alarm.

On reaching town he does not wait,
But rides straight through the city gate.
He marches to the Temple Mount,
Tips up the boards of those who count.
Ill-gotten gains through shady means.
He drives out cattle from the scene.
"This is my Father's house," he shouts.
As all the merchants he drives out.
"My Father's house," he shouts again,
"But you've made it a robbers' den."

The King has ridden here to die.
Some in the crowd shout "Crucify."
A vicious bandit they release.
The King's ordeal – it does not cease.
For several hours it is extended,

Until the King cries, "It is ended."
What he'd intended he had done,
On the cross the victory won.
He had conquered death and sin,
That all to heaven might enter in.

For death could not confine the King.
So we may say, Death, where's your sting.
And where's your victory, O grave,
The King has come, and come to save.

Good News

Our God has loved us to such an extent;
His Son came to this world and to Calvary went.
He, on our behalf, on the cross His life spent
So that, if we believe him, and before Him repent,
Because of the price that for Jesus it cost,
He has given assurance that we shan't be lost.
He has, through the Gospel, allowed us to see
That we can be raised up eternally.
Lord Jesus, the Saviour, can do this for you
If Him you will trust as your Saviour too.
For God did not send Him the world to condemn.
But for those who have faith give salvation to them.

A Denier and Adonai

"Peter, you'll deny me three whole times
Before cock crow and morning chimes."
"The others, Lord, may fall away
But whatever happens with you I'll stay."

The beloved disciple took Peter higher
To warm himself beside the fire.
A servant girl who did Peter see
Said, "You were with Jesus of Galilee."

Peter at once denied it all
The first of the three times that he would fall.
As Peter edged slowly to leave through the gate
A second girl servant called him to wait,

"You were with Jesus, one of his crowd,"
But Peter insisted to all very loud
And standing up straight he started to spout
"I don't even know what you're talking about."

A third time a group of them came up to him
For Peter the outcome might be very grim.
You're from the Jesus of Nazareth gang
We know because of your Galilee twang.

Peter turned round and he cursed and he swore
To make sure he continued to do so some more.
Then all of a sudden, the cock started to crow
And Peter remembered Jesus said it would so.

Peter went out and he wept and he cried
For he knew that three times his Lord he'd denied.
Could he be forgiven? He doubted he could
For denying the Master outweighed any good.

Some weeks later Jesus, risen from the dead
Met Peter who'd gone back to fishing instead.
Jesus called him aside by the shore of the lake
And asked him some questions for Peter's own sake.

"Do you, Peter, love me more than all these
More than your fishing, more also than these,
The friends that you've been with a couple of years?"
And Peter looked back to the night he'd shed tears.

"Yes, Lord, you know that I love you indeed."
For Jesus' forgiveness he wanted to plead,
But Jesus told him, before he could start,
To feed Jesus' lambs. It reached Peter's heart.

A second time Jesus asked, "Simon of John,
Do you truly love me?" which he seized upon/
"You know I do truly," said he who could weep.
And Jesus replied then, "Take care of my sheep."

A third time asked Jesus of Peter the man
"Do you just love me?" Peter says what he can.
He's hurt by the question that Jesus has asked.
Says Jesus knows all things which includes his own past.

"You know that I love you; you know that I do."
Jesus looks back at Peter and quietly says to
The fisherman Peter to feed all his sheep
To care for his flock in safety to keep.

My God, Why?

My God, My God, Why?
Despised, rejected by men.
Take this cup from me.

My God, My God, Why?
Despised, rejected by men.
Yet your will be done.

My God, My God, Why?
Despised, rejected by men.
Father, forgive them.

My God, My God, Why?
Despised, rejected by men.
But it is finished.

My God, My God, Why?
Despised, rejected by me.
You still died for me.

Walkers and Talkers Walk
Back Up the Track

After midday at Easter a couple of friends
Were walking along the footpath that wends
Its way to Emmaus from Jerusalem town
But walking together with eyes looking down.
They talked to each other how Jesus had died
How Pontius Pilate had him crucified.
When as they were talking, a stranger jogged by
And asked why they looked almost likely to cry.
"Are you but a stranger in the city this week?
For us and our kindred the future seems bleak.
The one we expected to be our true guide
Was captured and taken to be crucified."
The stranger then told them just how they were blind
And proceeded to tell them they should bring to mind
The prophets from scripture who spoke of a king
Who would suffer, a servant, salvation to bring.
And starting from Adam went all the way through,
Through Isaiah, Zechariah and Psalm 22.

He spoke about Moses being given the Law,
The Passover, Abraham and an awful lot more.
And finally, when the light became dim,
How the Law and the Prophets all pointed to him.
They came to an inn when it began to get dark

The stranger appeared to continue his walk.
The friends him persuaded to stay for a rest.
The stranger took bread and wine which he blessed.
At once both the friends, when he lifted the bread
Recognised Jesus, alive from the dead.
The friends then rushed back and when they arrived
Told all the disciples the Lord is alive.

Lockdown and Didymus

Disciples locked in an upper room
Their mood was one of gloom and doom.
They all knew their Lord had died,
Upon the cross been crucified.

But he had risen from the tomb
And there he was within the room.
When Jesus said, "Be with you peace."
Their gloom immediately ceased.
Their sadness turned at once to joy
With him who powers of death destroyed.
"Just as the Father has sent me,
So I send you witness to be."
And he who passed to life from death
Breathed on disciples with his breath
"Receive the Holy Ghost," said he.
"Sins you forgive, forgiven will be."

Now Thomas was not with the rest
When Jesus all the others blessed.
The others said Jesus had risen
For Tom he faced a new decision
He'd not believe his Lord had risen
Unless he could within the incision
Of the nails and in the side

Place his fingers right inside.
Next Sunday Tom, still in his gloom,
When Jesus came into the room.
He came to Thomas called the twin
And said to put his finger in
The holes where all the nails had been.
But Thomas having Jesus seen,
No need for nail holes he would prod,
Said to his Lord, "My Lord and God."
Thomas' doubts had been found out.
So Jesus said, "Believe, don't doubt."
Tom believed 'cos he had seen.
Blessed be those, not seen, had been.

Pentecost

At Pentecost the Spirit came
With mighty wind and tongues of flame.
In the holy city were many races
Many tongues and many faces.
They all heard the Word of God
Proclaimed in their own native tongue.
To them it seemed to be quite odd
In their own language to hear God's song.
People there who came from Crete,
Parthians, Elamites and Medes
And those who'd left Cyrene's heat
All could hear God's mighty deeds.
Strangers too who'd left their home
And travelled all the way from Rome
Could hear the words that Peter spoke
When he spoke out to all the folks.
Some suggested they were drunk
But Peter said that that was bunk.
This accusation he could mock
By saying it's just nine o'clock.
Then Peter started to explain
That by them Jesus had been slain.
For all the world Jesus had bled
But then had risen from the dead.
But in the last days God would pour

His Spirit out on rich and poor,
His servants would receive the Spirit
Whose gifts and fruit they would inherit.
And when the Holy Spirit came
All who called upon God's name
The Lord to them the Spirit gave
And by the Lord they all were saved.

Luke and See

Honours should be Doctor Luke's
For writing for us his two books.
His Gospel and the Book of Acts
Provide for us the detailed facts
Of Jesus' life and that of Paul
For Luke it is who gives them all.
With Paul imprisoned in Caesarea
Luke began a new career
Prepared to write down without fear.
What from Christians he did hear
All that Jesus did and said
And how he'd risen from the dead.
As doctor, Luke could know the feeling
Of those who needed Jesus' healing.
In his Gospel Luke is reaching
Readers with the Saviour's teaching.
To bring to light things from the dark
Which Luke could borrow from St Mark.
In reading Luke we see his worth
For details of the Saviour's birth.
Through his writing to Theophilus
May the Spirit come and so fill us.

The Word Applied
Comes Before a Fall

How long should a sermon be?
With one point or the standard three?
Should it continue hours and hours
Include of blessings many showers?
Example for new preachers all
Is for them the apostle Paul.
When for breaking bread they met,
What a sermon they did get.
Starting when the sun first shone
Paul's sermon just went on and on.
So long that suffering with a cough
One Eutychus had nodded off.
Seated in a window space
He'd heard Paul speak about God's grace.
But after listening in the main
He leant back on the window pane.
Thinking of things Paul spoke about
He leant too far and toppled out.
From storey three he hit the ground
And made a rather banging sound.
Those present all rushed down to see
And all believed that dead was he.
Paul threw himself upon the lad
And then said, "Do not be alarmed

Despite his fall he isn't harmed.
Though falling from above the ceiling
He will be well with Jesus' healing."
And all the people there were glad
They'd thought that Eutychus was dead
But Paul went back and broke the bread.
As next day Paul would sail away
He kept on preaching while he may.
When Paul was speaking all the while
They took the lad to his domicile.
Paul continued preaching right
Until the middle of the night.
Those present all moved to be near
So keen they were St Paul to hear.
So preachers preaching long and deep
Be careful lest some fall asleep.
Don't have a hearer fall down dead
Expound the good news well instead.
For everyone whom Paul had heard
With joy had heard him preach God's word.

A Useful Letter

Dear Philemon, I am Paul.
I'm writing you this little letter
I know to meet you would be better
I'm sorry that I cannot call.

I write to ask from you a favour
Knowing you're a kindly slaver.
In asking you I must be brave
To ask you to release a slave.

When on my travels far from home
As prisoner I arrived in Rome.
And when I needed help it came
By slave, Onesimus by name.

Onesimus his story gave
He said that he had been your slave.
But when he feared you one fine day
He upped and left and ran away.

Like many slaves he fled to Rome
And since he came, it's been his home.
In Rome he's altered his behaviour,
Found Jesus as his Lord and Saviour.

His name I understand means useful.
To you he wasn't very truthful
In fact quite useless proved to be;
But then so useful was to me.

I said to him he must return.
To serve you rightly he must learn.
He's now become a Christian brother
I beg you treat him as another.

One thing more I'd like to say
Can I remind you if I may?
It's something that I'm sure you'll see.
You're a Christian thanks to me.

I've never asked you; may I show
Eternal life to me you owe.
And so, Philemon, I request
Please take him back, you'll both be blessed.

A Pair of Golden Eagles and a Sun

Priscilla and Aquila were Jews who'd lived in Rome.
When ordered out by Claudius, in Corinth made their home.
Aquila was the husband, Priscilla was the wife
And both of them to Jesus had offered up their life

They met St Paul in Corinth when to that town he went
Their occupation, like St Paul's, was spent in making tents.
Although in making tents was a livelihood for each.
They bore the load of tent-making so that St Paul could preach.

When Paul had stayed some time with them, he felt he should move on
Priscilla and Aquila, too, by ship with him were gone.
They settled next in Ephesus and opened up their home
To all who loved the Lord of life, just as they'd done in Rome.

Among their many visitors an Alexandrian came.
A learned man, quite erudite, Apollos was his name.
A Jew, he knew the Scriptures well, spoke boldly to the Jews,
And spoke to them of Jesus Christ, proclaiming the good news.

He only knew the baptism of John when he was here.
The couple took him to their home to make the way more clear.

Apollos, to evangelise, then sought to go to Greece,
The brothers here in Ephesus sent him there with their peace.
He came in Greece to Corinth and for brethren there did search,
And while he lived in Corinth was a great help to the church.

And what more do we know about Aquila and his wife?
St Paul can tell the Romans that for him they risked their life.
At length they moved from Ephesus, returning home to Rome,
And once again they led a group of Christians in their home.

What do the couple have to say to Christian folk today?
Like them we need to come together regularly to pray.
To open up our homes to our sisters and our brothers,
And also teach the Gospel fully to anybody other.

They moved around the Med working wherever they were able,
They shared the Gospel in their home and welcomed to their table.
They were prepared to risk their lives for persecuted Paul.
So we as well should show support for persecuted all.

So are our homes a place at which God's flock is always
greeted?
For both for meals and study time our friends are always
seated.
Do we have an Apollos to expound the Gospel whole,
To learn about the Spirit and how he lifts the soul?

A Royal Priesthood

As you come to Jesus, to the living stone,
Rejected by humanity, precious at God's own throne,
You too are being built, yourselves as living stones,
Alongside other Christians into a spiritual home,
To be a holy priesthood to offer unto God,
Sacrifices spiritual through Jesus Christ, your Lord,
Sacrifices spiritual acceptable to God.

You are a chosen people; for you belong to God.
You are a holy nation where all the saints have trod.
You are a royal priesthood to offer up God's praise,
For you are God's own people to worship all your days.

For you were called from darkness into God's glorious light.
You'd not received God's mercy, while you were still in
night.
But now you know God's mercy to save you from sin's
mire,
So live life not as pagans; abstain from sin's desires.
So pagan folk who see you and see what you have done,
May come to God to glorify the day when he will come.
For like a missing ewe lamb you had wandered from the
fold,
But now you have returned to the Shepherd of your soul.

The Man with a Lamp

To the angel of the church in Laodicea
What the Spirit says you need to hear.
Hear the Amen's explanation.
He who rules all God's creation,
He the witness faithful and true.
Listen to what he says about you.
He knows your deeds, would you were hot,
But he himself knows that you are not.
He knows your deeds, would you were bold,
But he knows neither are you cold.
Would that you then were one or the other,
When acting as Christ's sister or brother.
But he knows your current form.
Instead you only are lukewarm.
He to you would wish to shout,
As you're lukewarm, I'll spew you out.
You say always something which,
Confirms to all that you are rich.
You tell us all that you are wealthy,
What you say you think is healthy,
You to all are keen to sing,
That you've no need of anything.
The trouble is there is a flaw.
You're wretched, pitiful and poor.
You cannot see that you are blind,

That naked too He you will find.
So buy from Him gold to acquire,
Which He's refined within the fire.
Thereby you may indeed be rich.
And whereas now you've not a stitch,
You'll wear white clothes for all to see.
Put salve on your eyes so you can see.
Those whom he loves He will reprove
And discipline them to make them move,
So that they then start to repent.
For all the wasted time they've spent.
I, the Amen, stand at the door,
And knock and wait for some time more.
Whoever hears me and opens up,
I will go in and with him sup.
To any who's able to overcome, rather,
I'll give them the right to sit on my throne.
As I overcame and sat down on my Father's.
Let all with an ear hear the Spirit's own tone.

Sorry!

Since I was a kid, what I shouldn't, I did.
Despite what I wished, into sin I soon slid.
And if it was possible, my sins I then hid.
Forgive me, O Lord, I'm a sinner.

Of my sins there's a lot; what I should, I did not,
Of sins that I did, some were cold and some hot.
And if someone saw me, I hoped they'd not spot.
Forgive me, O Lord, I'm a sinner.

I try to repent, but I'm still a beginner,
Outwardly fine, but ashamed of my inner.
Forgive me, O Lord, I'm a sinner.

In anger I've driven too fast on through Chinnor,
And just missed a car when passing through Pinner.
Forgive me, O Lord, I'm a sinner.

In Europe I once nearly hit a Berliner.
Of requests through the post I'm a very good binner.
Forgive me, O Lord, I'm a sinner.

When someone slips up, I regret I'm a grinner.
In trouble as well, I'm a tall tale type of spinner.
Forgive me, O Lord, I'm a sinner.

I eat far too much when I'm having my dinner,
As I'm not a cook, I'm an open a tinner.
So I'm far too fat when I should have been thinner.
Forgive me, O Lord, I'm a sinner.

I'd best not repeat all the sins on my sheet,
Maybe known on the street!
I acknowledge defeat.
Forgive me, O Lord, I'm a sinner.

So I've come to repent for the time I've misspent
To indulgence I went.
Though that's not what I meant.
Forgive me, O Lord, I'm a sinner.

At the cross, Lord, I know that you were the winner.
And so, dear Lord, though I am still a beginner
Through your mercy and grace I'm a forgiven sinner.

I Wish

I wish I'd been evangelist bringing others to the Lord;
I wish I'd been a preacher who could wield the Spirit's
sword;
I wish I'd been a teacher with scripture knowledge deep;
I wish I'd been a pastor who could care for Jesus' sheep;
I wish I'd been a prophet with a word that came from God;
I wish I'd walked the pathway on which the Lord has trod;
I wish I'd been a missionary telling people overseas;
I wish I'd been a pray-er spending longer on my knees.
I know I'm not a one of them, but my spirit swiftly soared
When the Saviour did enlist me in Dad's Army of the Lord.

A Not Very Pretty Ditty for Faith in Our City

Lord, we ask for Christian unity
That we may have the opportunity
To spread the gospel with immunity
Not with any importunity
With the whole of our humanity
Especially in our own community
And may we work in unanimity
And speak the word with equanimity
But proclaim with great humility
In the power of God's authority
Through Jesus Christ who has deity
By faith they may have life for eternity,
Whether rich and those who suffer paucity,
Where there may be of food a scarcity
For those who go to university
Whatever their background through diversity
Including where they face adversity.
May God bless our town and any worse city.

Last Question

I'm approaching the end of my innings;
So it's time for a brand new beginning.
I need to repent
For the time I've misspent
And for all of the time spent in sinning.

Before you, Lord, I'll face a test.
I'll claim that I've just done my best.
But to win your election
You require full perfection
As a condition to enter your rest.

I know when I look at the stuff
That I've done in my life's not enough
For what is required
To avoid the hell fire.
My deeds you may count as mere fluff.

Yet, Lord, you've provided a way
For Jesus for our sins did pay.
For once on the cross
He paid for our loss
So to enter to heaven we may.

So I'll come before God to repent
For us through the Son that he sent.
In his mercy and grace
We'll see Him face to face,
The Saviour whose life for us spent.

So now in my life that remains
I'll take action to wipe out the stains
That have sullied my life
With sin, anger and strife
Through what Jesus has done for our gain.

So the thing that God says that we must
Before our old bodies are dust,
For by faith alone
We can come to God's throne,
In Jesus to put all our trust.

It's not then in life what we do
That will see us to heaven pass through.
Trust good deeds is fraud.
It's true faith in the Lord
That is open for me and for you.

May we ask you this question once more?
Of salvation can you be sure?
Trusting Jesus as Saviour,
Not your own behaviour,
And follow Christ Jesus as Lord?
Are you certain that you are forgiven?
Your place is reserved up in heaven?

So raised to the height
In the Kingdom of Light
In the new body that you'll be given.

So if you're not sure, let me say
There's one simple way you can pray.
"Lord, I'm in a spin,
Please forgive all my sin
For Jesus my sentence did pay."

Come Back Together in Jesus' Name

Lord, we bring to you in prayer
The NHS and social care.
We come to you because we feel
That you, Lord, are the one to heal.
We pray the covid-19 virus
Will very soon no longer tire us.
Lord, please do take away our fears
And thank you for the volunteers
Who shop for us in several stores
And say to us, "Yes, it is yours."
Please bless our local surgeries
And those who work there as GPs.
Lord, you are the great physician
We pray for all whatever position
They hold within the NHS
We ask, dear Lord, that you will bless.
In hospital or pharmacy
And those who bring round cups of tea.
One thing special, Lord, we ask,
Lord, please arrange to get some masks.
Doctors, nurses all we see
Have been in need of PPE.
For those who need intensive care
We offer up a special prayer.

We pray as well for those who grieve
Because by COVID they're bereaved.
We pray for those long shut indoors
And those who help them with their chores.
Our list of prayers continues but
We think of schools that had to shut.
We thank you, Lord, for all the action
Leading to produce a vaccine
For all who worked within the lab
So we could all receive a jab.
Each Sunday while we may not meet
And one another cannot greet.
But as a light within the gloom
We come together by means of Zoom.
We've virtually met for prayer and praise
And done so now 200 days.
But what a joy it then will be
When face to face we each can see.
And in each church within the Parish
We'll celebrate in Langley Marish.
So, when we meet, we shall be giving,
You, Lord, our sincere thanksgiving.
And then at last we'll reach the date
When together we can celebrate.
To share in worship and in praise
To bring petitions; God's name to raise.
To hear God's Word as it is read;
To share the Creed as it is said.
To meet below the cross, our sign,
And share Communion bread and wine.
To show God's love as peace we share

To show God's people that we care.
So, let us all in praise unite
As we come together to spread God's light.

A 21st Century Amos 4

You English bullies crush those in need
And to the Lord you give no heed.
You go to church but there you sin
Announce how much you've handed in.

You women who oppress the poor
And drinking wine just ask for more.
The Sovereign Lord's time it will come
You'll face the music, that and some.

I shook the sea and rocked the land
With earthquakes down in New Zealand.
As a warning you could see
Yet you have not returned to me.

The summer's heat – 40 degrees
And with no hint of cooling breeze.
As a warning you could see.
Yet you have not returned to me.

Ravenous locusts now swarming much thicker
Denuding the crops, spread across Africa.
As a warning you could see
Yet you have not returned to me.

Fires burned across Australia
With flames being fanned when the winds were much galier
As a warning you could see
Yet you have not returned to me.

The rain drops from clouds when it has its warrant
Last year the rain, it came down in torrents.
As a warning you could see.
Yet you have not returned to me.

The dams and defences proved to be duds
When the Aire, Severn and Wye all spread out as floods.
As a warning you could see.
Yet you have not returned to me.

You have permitted now to mire us
With the dreadful coronavirus.
As a warning you can see.
Still you have not returned to me.

Therefore, this is what I'll do.
And, what I'll do, I'll do to you.
You look to see the Day of the Lord
But away into exile I'll send you abroad.
Until on that day, the Day of the Lord,
My people from exile will all be restored,

Search for a Church

As in Christ I've found salvation
I have started now to search
To find a good denomination
So I can join a lively church.
Of the Gospel I know the gist.
Should I become a Methodist?
Some people think that I am barmy
Not joining the Salvation Army.
With no baptism, is there a gap missed?
So I should now become a Baptist.
Of course, I now instead could be
A member of the URC.
Surely I could find a home
Within the Catholic Church of Rome.
Or also, bless my cotton socks,
I'd join the Russian Orthodox.
Seeking advice, a person gave one
That I should be a new Moravian.
And, of course, a not inferior one,
I should become a Presbyterian.
Others met me in a hostel
And said I should be Pentecostal.
Though I am a simple bod.
I'd join an Assembly of God.
Or as at present I am feeling

Should I join up at an Elim?
Or leave the others in the lurch
And find an FIEC church.
If I went forward and stopped my blethering
Could I join the Christian Brethren?
Or could I come to meet my Maker
And as a Friend become a Quaker?
Or if I followed a German man
I could become a Lutheran.
Or where believers should agree
By attending at an LEP.
There's still the good old C of E
Of belief and practice I can see;
It could be high and bow and scrape,
Or in the middle not awake,
Or as a modern filled with doubting,
Or evangelical – gospel shouting.
A church that's there through history
Or else a plant from HTB.
Some folks who come will just insist
They've come to Solemn Eucharist.
Others say, if they are able,
They've come to meet round the Lord's Table.
Wherever I go I want the sense
In worship of our God's presence.
And whether we say or sing a hymn
I know that we'll have worshipped Him.
I simply want to serve my Lord
With one desire and one accord.
Please tell me now where I should be
For him who died and rose for me.

Prayer Comes the Rain

For many months there'd been no rain
The farmers started to complain.
The fields were dry throughout the nation
The church gave farmers intimation.
That on the Sunday called Rogation
The Vicar and the congregation.
Would come into the farmers' fields
To pray for rain and pray for yields.
So on that Sunday half past two
The Vicar, choir and others who.
Had come to join the time of prayer
Processed from church to fields quite bare.
They walked along a little lane
So at the farm could pray for rain.
The farmers wanted to oblige a
Group of pray-ers like Elijah.
When in the field they came together
They looked to see what type of weather.
Looking up, the skies were blue
The sun was shining hotly too.
The Vicar started leading prayer
To God who for all folks takes care.
Please, Lord, we pray to you for rain
The farmers all are under strain.
We pray they'll have a decent yield

From crops they're planting in these fields.
Although this year the fields look blank
May we at harvest come with thanks.
On Monday morning came the rain
From then on rain did never stop.
It soaked the fields and grew the grain
The once dry fields they copped the lot.
When harvest came what celebration
In the church's congregation.
All rejoiced and gave God thanks
For cabbages the size of tanks.
It showed that when to God we pray
He'll hear and answer right away.
Out in the fields amazed were all
To see that maize was eight foot tall.
For when we joined in prayer from Copp
The Lord provided such a crop.

On the Lord's Hill

Some services gave a special thrill,
While worshipping upon Lord's Hill.
Especially I can still remember,
Spring and summer and December.

Our springtime service, Easter 2,
Might be of interest to you.
Passover was our service theme,
To see what happened, how it seemed.
We brought along a leg of lamb,
The real thing, not tin of spam.
The lamb we brought was soaked in blood,
Though not enough to cause a flood.
Instead we took the blood outside,
The children then, before it dried.
Took out a cloth with blood still wet,
We adults then the children let.
To wipe two doorposts with the gore,
And then they wiped a couple more.
Returning then to come inside,
They learned how sons not 'neath the blood.
That evening by death's angel died
But sprinkled with Lord Jesus' blood.
We all may conquer death and grave,
Through Jesus who came us to save.

The summer theme – feeding 5k,
To avoid them being sent away.
One member brought 5 little buns,
Two sardine tins sold each in ones.
We circulated the buns and fish,
We'd put out on a little dish.
Each person present there could take,
And have some juice their thirst to slake.
And after everyone had eaten,
We saw how Jesus had hunger beaten.

December was a night of healing,
In prayer to Jesus we were kneeling.
We prayed for Sarah five years old,
The next week due an operation.
With God and medics co-operation,
In prayer for healing we were bold.
God our intercession heeded,
The operation was not needed.
Our trust in Jesus further sealed,
Her problem ear already healed.
An anxious lady came to pray,
Her sister was so very ill.
Her chance of living almost nil,
Unlikely she would last ten days.
Our congregation from different lands,
For her we prayed and laid on hands.
The prayer that night anxiety eased,
Her sister died next week in peace.

Dieu, Je T'en Prie

What is this life if, full of care,
We take no time to spend in prayer.
No time to bring concerns to God,
Which for a Christian seems quite odd.
As we're so busy all our days,
We take no time to give God praise.
Our diaries have so few times blank,
No time to offer up our thanks.
No time to come and sing a hymn,
To show to God our love for Him.
No time to read a Gospel verse,
Or alms to give from out our purse.
Dear Lord, forgive us that we fail,
To come to greet you with "All hail!"
No time to feel your grace and love,
You pour on us as from above.
We ask that you will give us time,
That we to heaven in prayer may climb.
You taught disciples how to pray,
Please teach us too how prayer to say.
A poor life this if, full of care,
We have no time to come in prayer.

Silver and Gold

God's work done God's way.
Will not want for God's supplies.
Do it to prove it.

No silver or gold.
But in Jesus' name now walk.
He walked, jumped, praised God.

No silver or gold.
Spend night with someone worthy.
Bring peace to their home.

Macedonians.
Gave Paul a contribution.
To support the saints.

How much will British.
Support their persecuted.
Brothers and sisters?

To seek the newborn.
Wise men still come from the east.
Even from China.

Pay tax to Caesar.
Pay HMRC what's due.
What's God's? Pay Him too.

It Is as Easy in
St Francis of Assisi

If one day you come to research
What happens at St Francis Church.
You'd find each Sunday morn we meet
And if you came, we you would greet.
We meet most Sundays half past nine
To share Communion bread and wine.
But each fourth Sunday at eleven
We meet to praise the Lord in heaven.
Each week we wonder who'll
Join us upstairs at Sunday School.
On Wednesday's we come here at ten
To share the bread and wine again.
And when we've shared the bread and wine
We meet in a group of roughly nine.
To read the Bible and discuss
What the passage means for us.
So we can know for evermore
Our Bible studies teach us more.
About salvation through the Lord
The word of God – the Spirit's sword.
On Thursdays once a month we meet
For tea and cakes, o what a treat.
Come to "Refresh" if you're a seeker
To have some tea and hear a speaker.

Though designed for older folks
We're pleased to greet some other blokes.
Round a table you may sit
And meet with friends and chat a bit.
Every Friday "Little Flowers
Of St Francis" so they're ours.
We have a time of play before
Our story time then sing once more.

Little Flowers should not be missed
But sadly there's a waiting list.
We're open to parents and those too who care
We'll invite you along when capacity's spare.
Each Summer Holiday at Home
For older folks who cannot roam.
Abroad on holiday away
But each instead at home must stay.
There's indoor games and jigsaws too
A trip outside we also do.
You could try painting or another craft
And entertainment at which you'll laugh.
We have a library from which to borrow
That so few do is a cause of sorrow.
Once a quarter we read a set book
And at what it tells us we all of us look.
Each weekday morning we come to pray –
For a different road and its people each day.
We pray for healing for those who are ill
And comfort for those who are grieving still.
One Saturday each year in July or June
We offer some scones, jam, a jar and a spoon.

To all passers-by through our grounds – it's for free
So all can enjoy a heavenly cream tea.
We have a garden with a comfortable seat
We have a building where each week we meet.
When we don't need it, the building's for hire
But at worship we ask God to set us on fire.
So if you come down along Upton Court
And pass by our building, please give a thought.
To what goes on each week in our hall
It may be some time that you'll stop and you'll call.
You'll always be welcome when we you will meet
You're welcome as well if you sit on the seat.
You may stop and then ponder in our little garden
And we trust from your sins you'll encounter God's pardon.
So we invite you who read this to come in and meet
We'd love the occasion when we you could greet.
We hope you'll come here from whatever nation
So please come and join us in our congregation.

The Night Shelter

On a cold winter's night you may sometimes think how
To make best provision for the homeless in Slough.
May I bring to your notice that just out of sight
There's a shelter providing a home for the night.

For if near the High Street the cold you will feel
You can come and be given a hot tasty meal.
And when you have woken shortly before dawning
We'll give you a breakfast to start off your morning.

Could we suggest that there's something all oughta
Become of the charity a good will supporter.
Some years ago the scheme was begun
So examine the web of London and Slough Run.

Lent

It's Lent
Is it Lent?
What is Lent?
If it's 'Lent',
Someone must have borrowed it.
40 days by God are Lent.
40 days someone has borrowed.
Why?
God lends us time,
Time to choose.
Time to spend with him.
Time to face the test.
Time to face the accuser.
Time to reject the evil one.
Time to find true bread of life.
Time to reject all personal power.
Time not to put God to the test.
After 40 days, return what's borrowed.
After 40 days return what's Lent.
After 40 days we come to Easter
So we no longer need to borrow.
He no longer needs to lend.
As we and our time have both been paid for.

He's Coming

He's coming.
Is he?
Who's coming?
He is.
Who's he?
Well, you know.
The Alpha and the Omega.
Where's he coming?
Here.
Where's he coming from?
Where he is now.
When's he coming?
I'm not sure, but I know he's coming; coming here.
You need to be ready.
What for?
For when he comes.
How do you know he's coming?
Because he told us,
What did he say?
He said that he was coming back.
You need to be ready.
He may come when he's not expected.
So why should I start to prepare?
In case you miss him when he does come.
Are you sure he's coming?

Yes, because he said so.

Did you believe him when he said he was coming?

Yes, because what he says is true.

So what do you think I should do?

Get ready.

How?

Well, you know. What would you do if you knew he was coming?

Go out to see who he was.

Well, why not do so now?

Because I don't where and when or even who.

But when you see him coming, you'll know.

But what if he doesn't come?

He will.

Should I wait until he's near?

No because while he's on his way, you might miss him.

He might miss me.

He won't.

How do you know?

Because I know him.

Why would he want to see us?

Because that's his way.

What about the others?

They need to be prepared too.

What if they all want to see him?

Every eye will see him.

Perhaps you should do something now so you can't miss him.

What sort of thing?

You could always climb a tree!

What, me?

Yes, you.

And get ready in case he wants to stay with you.

Not me. He won't want to talk to me. You know me and what I am.

But He is coming.

When, again?

Soon. So, get ready!

9 781398 442740